Cooking is Fun

Afro-Caribbean style

To,

Diane

OXO

a weekend cooking project with friends

Grace Aderonke Adegoke

Published by HGA – HIS Grace Alone Publisher

Published by HGA – HIS Grace Alone Publisher

All rights reserved

For information,
Address: HGA, Claremond, Storeton Village
Wirral, CH63 6HW
England
www.rnk-foods.co.uk
www.graceadegoke.co.uk

ISBN 978-0-9563497-0-5

Design & Photographs by Grace Aderonke Adegoke
Produced by PACE Image & Print
Printed in England

Contents

Acknowledgements

I am grateful to everyone who has been a source of
encouragement to me along the way in making this a
reality.

My heartfelt thanks to all my family and friends and also
my customers who enjoy my cooking.

My neighbour and friend Katerina for support, proof
reading and editing also, to Garth, Bill and all the team at
Pace Image & Print, for their willingness and readiness to
work with me at all times. Most importantly to God
almighty who gives me strength.

Dedication

This piece is dedicated to the loving memories of both my grandmothers, whose lives, influence, incredible tenacity and talents, rubbed off on me.

Two beautiful women
Maria Ajadi and Esther Oyerele.

Foreword

The idea for this Afro-Caribbean cookery book was conceived last autumn when Grace decided she would put pen to paper and produce a splendid book, full of mouthwatering recipes with easy to prepare, new flavours and tasty different recipes to try with your friends, with the accent on very "healthy" good quality ingredients.

Grace has written and illustrated her own menus just for you, with the inclusion of her very own professional photographs.

Despite being the owner of a very successful Afro-Caribbean restaurant the very talented and dynamic Grace has found the time to write and produce this wonderful cookery book.

From the moment you start collecting your ingredients, you can forget the hassles and mystique about any difficulties preparing Caribbean food. Grace will show you how it is done with her easy steps and techniques that really work so you will soon feel confident as you make these delicious "healthy" recipes.

I hope people will see this book as one that you can pick up and know that you will find something you want to make. The recipes are easy to follow, straight forward and don't take long to prepare.

I hope you will take the time and have some fun "Cooking with Friends" and enjoy the wonders and delights of some really truly "healthy" wonderful new and exciting ideas for all your family and friends.

Katerina Palios

Introduction

This book is borne out of passion for cooking and teaching people how to cook which is something I have always loved. Also as a result of my friends and customers who have tasted my cooking asking me to teach them how to cook. I hope you find this book useful and interesting.

If you can't make a real life journey to the Colourful Caribbean or the stunning and diverse Africa, you can still sample the flavours and experience the culinary delights right there in your own home. Why don't you gather a few friends and get cooking following these simple easy to use recipes.

"So imagine yourself on a sunny beach, with the sparkly Caribbean lapping gently on the sand, a steel band playing softly in the distance and the glorious tastes of the tropics surrounding you."

This is the story about this style of cooking.

In the 19th century, the great melting pot of the Caribbean was complete. Labourers, merchants and traders (in the slave trade) from all over the world: Spanish, French, Africans, Scots, Irish, English, Dutch, Indians and Chinese all brought their music, their sport, their language and cooking styles, merging into a riot of colour sunshine.

The extensive use of spices makes Caribbean food lively and different; this is largely due to the fact that the African slaves grew tired of the plain boring basic food they were given, so they made it palatable with a hefty sprinkling of locally grown spices.
The continent of Africa is enormous. There is great diversity in culture, tribes and languages.

In many AFRICAN countries, from Algeria to Zimbabwe, cooking is a social event; the journey to the market, picking up fresh ingredients for the cooking, everyone in the family (especially women) taking part in the cooking. All these activities give them the chance to talk, chill out and have fun making cooking a pleasurable experience rather than a chore.

Most of all, African and Caribbean cooking is about freshly cooked meals using fresh ingredients mostly organic, local and non processed.

How to use this book

You might have read in the introduction that this style of cooking is about cooking with fresh ingredients. To cook most of the recipes here, you need some ingredients from the ethnic stores, or even your local supermarket especially in the big cities.

The main ingredients have been photographed alongside each recipe, so you can identify what you need to buy at the store especially if you are not familiar with them.

You need basic kitchen utensils, a domestic food processor and some pans. You do not need any fancy gadgets. Also, you do not need a weighing scale, I tried to give different style measurements to suit what you are cooking. Some ingredients come pre packed already measured for you, some you need to measure.

The recipes can be tweaked or adjusted to suit your own taste. Some of the recipes take some time to prepare, hence I have catered in the recipes so that you can serve a large number of people and you can just freeze the rest in sizeable portions. Most of these will freeze for months.

So what are you waiting for?
Get a few friends together and get cooking!

Yam Pepper Soup

Preparation time: 15 minutes
Cooking time: 30 minutes
Serves: 2-4

INGREDIENTS
- Yam (cut and peel about 6 slices, more yam if main course)
- Fish (or beef, oxtail, assorted meat, or vegetables, as much as you want)
  (use butternut squash, courgette and carrot, mixed peppers for vegetarian option, cut into chunks)
- Onions x1 small (diced)
- Tomato Puree x 1 tablespoon
- Fresh coriander (chopped) x 1 handful
- Palm oil x 1 tablespoon
- Salt and seasoning cubes
- Other spices – thyme, all purpose spice (or pre packed pepper soup mix) or whatever you have in the cupboard!
- Chilli or scotch bonnet pepper (to taste, chopped)

METHOD OF COOKING
- Boil your meat until soft (season to taste)
- Add peeled yam, onion, mixed peppers, chilli, and tomato puree, palm oil
- Add fresh fish or vegetables (If using fish or veg. option)
- Season to taste
- Simmer for about 10-15 mins
- Finally add your freshly chopped coriander

SERVING SUGGESTION
Serve piping hot (as a starter or main course)

er Soup

Ackee and White Fish

Preparation time: 30 minutes
Cooking time: 20 minutes
Serves: 2-3

INGREDIENTS

- Ackee x 1 can (drained) 400g
- White fish (fresh) or well rinsed and flaked salt fish (cod) x 500g
  (To rinse the salt fish, soak overnight, drain the water about four times.
  Boil for a few minutes, rinse off salt completely, remove bones, and flake.)
- Onions x 1 small (diced)
- Plum tomatoes (x 4 fresh chopped or half of a small can)
- Mixed pepper (fresh, a quarter of each colour diced)
- Fresh coriander (chopped)
- Sunflower oil x 2 tablespoons
- Salt and seasoning cubes
- Other spices – thyme, all spice, all purpose seasoning or whatever you have in the cupboard!
- Chilli or scotch bonnet pepper (to taste, chopped)

METHOD OF COOKING

- Pour the oil in the pan
- Stir fry your onion, mixed peppers, chilli, and plum tomatoes
- Mix in the flaked salt fish or steamed white fish (If raw allow about 5 minutes to cook)
- Season to taste
- Gently stir in the drained ackee
- Finally add your freshly chopped coriander

SERVING SUGGESTION

Serve with rice, bread fruit or plantain boiled, fried or roasted

white fish

Moin-Moin

(Steamed savoury bean cake)

Preparation time: 45 minutes
Cooking time: 40 - 60 minutes
Serves: 8-12

INGREDIENTS

- Peeled black eye beans (soaked in water for about 25 minutes or until soft) x 4 cups
- Big red sweet peppers x 4
- Medium sized onions x 4
- Scotch bonnet pepper or chilli x 1 (or to taste)
- Sunflower oil or palm oil x quarter cup
- Smoked African prawn or crayfish (whole or ground) x quarter cup
- Tinned Mackerel in sunflower oil or fresh and steamed (120g)
- Salt (to taste)
- Seasoning cubes to taste
- Hard boiled eggs (sliced for garnishing)
- Small to medium tin foil trays with cover x 24 (or more)

METHOD OF COOKING

- Rinse the pre-soaked soft beans until clear (soft enough when it's easy to break)
- Peel onions, wash peppers
- Blend together the beans, peppers and onion in a liquidizer, add water to liquidize to a soft paste or consistency (not too runny)
- Flake the mackerel
- Rinse the prawn or crayfish (if whole) in hot salted water (only use the fleshy part, take the head off the prawn)
- Add the oil, the rinsed cray fish, flaked mackerel, seasoning and salt to the liquidized beans
- Mix thoroughly and taste – adjust the seasoning to your taste
- Brush the tin foils with some of the vegetable oil, to prevent sticking
- Lay flat a slice of boiled egg on the bottom of the tin foil or in between or on top of the mixture
- Spoon out the mixture – (mix each time before spooning) into the tin foil, do not fill to the top, leave about 3 inches. Put the lid on the foil
- Systematically arrange each filled foil in a big pan with hot boiling water on the hob, making sure there is space behind each foil for steam to get to it. This arrangement will ensure your moin-moin is cooked quickly and evenly.

NOTE – omit fish and shrimps for vegetarian or vegan option

SERVING SUGGESTION
Serve with rice, bread, pap or eat alone

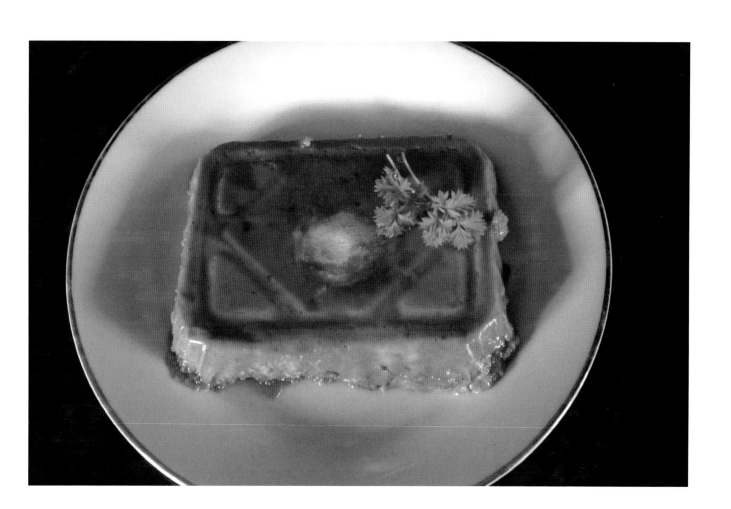

Vegetable Stew

Preparation time: 20 minutes
Cooking time: 30 minutes
Serves: 4-6

INGREDIENTS

- Fresh green vegetables x 2 big bunches or 1kg (fresh or frozen, traditional African vegetables; Efo Tete, Calalloo, cassava leaves, pumpkin leaves, spinach etc can be used). More than one vegetable can be combined
- Red Peppers x 2
- Plum tomatoes x 1 can or 6 fresh tomatoes
- Scotch bonnet pepper x 1 (optional for heat)
- Onions x 2 medium sized
- Spring Onions diced x 1 handful
- Palm oil x 4 tablespoons (or vegetable oil)
- Salt and seasoning cubes (to taste)
- Dry fish, crayfish - ground or whole, fresh fish, fresh meat, game etc – omit for vegetarian. As much as you want
- If using any meat or fish, boil first until soft before adding to the sauce
- Traditional African locust beans (Called Iru in Yoruba, Nigerian language). This is a fermented bean condiment used in really traditional West African cooking, this is optional

METHOD OF COOKING

- Chop all peppers, onions, and tomatoes (coarsely) in a food processor
- Slightly sauté some diced onions in the hot palm oil in a big pan
- Add the chopped ingredients and stir fry for about 10 – 15minutes. Do not add any water
- Add any fish or meat (already boiled until soft)
- Season to taste
- Cook until slightly dry and crispy
- Clean vegetables and slightly blanch in boiling water and chop
- Add the chopped vegetables to the pepper sauce
- Thoroughly stir, season if necessary. 3-5 minutes in the sauce, it's ready. Do not cook any longer

SERVING SUGGESTION

Serve with Rice, Pounded yam, Sadza etc

ble Stew

Pounded Yam

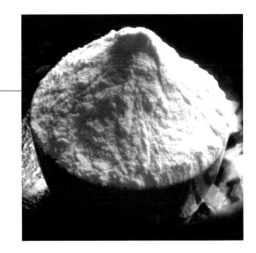

Preparation time: 1 minute
Cooking time: 15 minutes
Serves: 2-3

INGREDIENTS
- Water x 2 litres
- Yam powder 3-4 cups
- Wooden mixing spoon.

METHOD OF COOKING
- Boil some water in a pan (1.2 litres)
- Add some yam powder gradually into the boiling water and mix with the wooden spoon
- Add more powder until pliable like a soft dough
- Mix vigorously until smooth. Make sure there are no lumps!
- Add about 30ml hot water; simmer on lower heat for 3-5minutes
- Mix very well until water blends in (add more water if necessary, if too stiff)
- You need nice smooth, pliable soft dough
- Serve piping hot

SERVING SUGGESTION
Serve with Vegetable Stew, Okro stew, Ata sauce, Egusi, assorted meat / fish stew etc

a Yam

Ogbono Stew

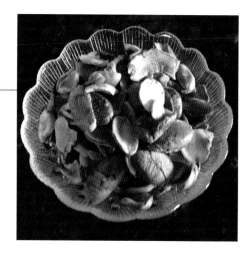

Preparation time: 35 minutes
Cooking time: 30 minutes
Serves: 6-8

INGREDIENTS
- Ogbono seed (in the picture above), or shop bought ground x 1 cup
- Grind the ogbono in a dry mill blender or grinder until smooth
- Assorted meat and fish, stock fish (as much as you want)
- Dry crayfish (whole or ground) half a cup
- Palm oil x 1 tablespoon
- Dry or fresh pepper (i.e chilli or scotch bonnet) to taste

METHOD OF COOKING
- Boil some assorted meats (whatever you want) until soft with loads of broths
- Add some pepper, fish, cray fish
- In a big bowl, pour the ground ogbono
- Slowly add some warm broth (about 1 litre) and mix with a big spoon until smooth (no lumps). Add a little broth at a time, as it has a tendency to be lumpy
- Add the ogbono paste into the whole mixture of meat and fish
- Add the palm oil
- Season and leave to cook for about 15-20 minutes until thick
- You can add some chopped okra or green vegetable for a richer and more nutritious stew. Add at the last few minutes of cooking

SERVING SUGGESTION
Serve with pounded Yam, Garri, Amala, Foofoo, Sadza

no Stew

Pepper Sauce

Preparation time: 15 minutes
Cooking time: 30 minutes
Serves: 8-10

INGREDIENTS
- Red Peppers x 3
- Plum tomatoes x 2 cans or fresh tomatoes
- Scotch bonnet pepper x 1 (picture above, optional for heat)
- Onions x 2 medium sized
- Vegetable oil x half cup
- Salt and seasoning cubes (to taste)
- Spices, i.e curry, thyme, etc
- Dry fish, fresh fish, fresh meat, game etc – omit for vegetarian. Use as much as you want
- If using any meat or fish, boil first until soft before adding to the sauce and simmer for a further 15 – 20 minutes

METHOD OF COOKING
- Chop all peppers, onions, and tomatoes in a blender (as smooth or coarse as you like)
- Slightly sauté some diced onions (about a handful) in the hot oil in a big pan
- Add the chopped ingredients and stir fry for about 10 – 15 minutes. Do not add any water
- Add any fish or meat (already boiled) and simmer for about 15 minutes
- Season to taste

SERVING SUGGESTION
Serve with rice, pounded yam, Sadza, bread or anything you fancy!

Sauce

Rice and Peas

Preparation time: 20 minutes
Cooking time: 30-40 minutes
Serves: 8-10

INGREDIENTS
- Easy Cook Rice x 6 cups
- Red kidney & Black Eye / Gungo Peas x 2 cups altogether
- Coconut Milk x 1 can (400g)
- Water x 6 cups
- Vegetable oil x 4 teaspoons (optional)
- Margarine x 3 teaspoons
- Fresh thyme x 4 sprigs
- Ground pimento x 2 teaspoons
- Ground Cumin x 1 teaspoon
- Chilli or Scotch Bonnet to taste (Ground or fresh)
- Peppercorn x 1 teaspoon
- Ginger x 1 teaspoon
- Salt x 2 teaspoons (to taste)
- Seasoning cubes x 2
- Diced fresh sweet peppers (different colours) x a quarter of each of green, red and yellow
- Fresh coriander

METHOD OF COOKING
- Using a fairly big pan
- Pour the water and the coconut milk into the pan (on the hob with full heat)
- Add the rest of the ingredients and all seasonings
- Wash the rice thoroughly under running water until clear and add to the ingredients
- Reduce the heat after about 6 minutes and stir together
- Let the rice cook for a total of about 20 minutes or so until soft to taste
- Add more water and seasoning if necessary
- Add the freshly diced peppers and chopped coriander 2 minutes before finishing

SERVING SUGGESTION
Garnish with fresh coriander
Serve with curried goat, jerk chicken, beef or fish, plantain for vegetarian option

and Peas

Jollof Rice

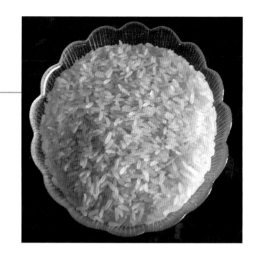

Preparation time: 20 minutes
Cooking time: 30 minutes
Serves: 6-8

INGREDIENTS

- Easy cook rice x 4 cups
- Plum tomatoes x 1 can (400g)
- Red Pepper x 2
- Vegetable oil x 4 tablespoon
- Margarine x 4 tablespoon
- Scotch Bonnet Pepper x1 (optional)
- Tomato puree x 200g
- Onion x 4 medium
- Thyme x 1 tablespoon
- Curry powder, mixed spice x half tablespoon each
- Salt and seasoning cubes to taste
- Chicken broth x 1 litre (use water for vegetarian option)
- Water x 1 litre

METHOD OF COOKING

- Blend the tomatoes, onions and peppers until smooth
- In a dry hot pan, add the vegetable oil and the margarine
- Saute some diced onions in the pan
- Add some mixed spice to the oil, stir fry for a minute
- Add the blend mixture of peppers, onions, tomatoes and tomato puree into the hot oil
- Add other spices, salt and seasoning cubes. Simmer for 5 minutes
- Add the chicken broth (also add meat or chicken if desired)
- Simmer for another 5 minutes, then clean the rice thoroughly and add
- Cook for a further 15-20 minutes or until rice is soft to your liking
- Adjust seasoning or water as necessary and stir thoroughly
- Finish cooking on very low heat during the last 10 or so minutes, Jollof rice has the tendency to burn very quickly

SERVING SUGGESTION

Serve with moin-moin, meat, fish, vegetables etc

Rice

Egusi Stew

Pumpkin – Like Seed (Melon)

Preparation time: 15 minutes
Cooking time: 30 minutes
Serves: 6-8

INGREDIENTS
- Ground egusi x 2 cups
- Meat or fish
- Crayfish, dry fish and smoked African prawn
- Red Peppers x 2
- Scotch bonnet x 1 optional
- Onions x 1 large
- Seasoning cubes and salt to taste
- Palm oil x 4 tablespoons
- African green vegetables x 1kg (or spinach)
- Locust beans (fermented bean condiment) optional

METHOD OF COOKING
- Boil the meat or fish until tender
- Grind the peppers and onions coarsely
- Add the meat to the pepper and onions in a pan with the meat broth
- Cook for about 5 minutes, then add the crayfish, smoked African prawn or dry fish and locust beans
- Add the ground egusi
- Add the palm oil
- Cook for a further 15 – 20 minutes
- Wash and chop the vegetables
- Add the vegetables in the last 5 minutes or so
- Season to taste

SERVING SUGGESTION
Serve hot with pounded yam, foofoo, Eba, Amala, white rice etc.

Maize Meal

Sadza / Ugali / Nshima

Preparation time: 5 minutes
Cooking time: 20-30 minutes
Serves: 4-6

INGREDIENTS

- Corn flour, white cornmeal or ground maize or millet flour x 5 cups
- Water
- Wooden spoon for mixing

METHOD OF COOKING

- Bring about 1.5 litres of water to the boil in a large pan
- Set aside 1 cup of the flour
- Place the remaining corn flour in a large bowl. Mix the corn flour with four cups of cold water
- Stir until the flour-water mixture is a thick paste
- Slowly add the flour-water paste to the boiling water, stirring constantly. Bring to a second boil, stirring constantly while the mixture thickens
- Do not allow lumps to form and do not allow it to stick to the bottom of the pot. Reduce the heat, cook and stir for a few minutes
- Slowly add the remaining flour. The mixture should be very thick and smooth
- Add a little water to steam and cook for a few minutes more
- Serve hot

SERVING SUGGESTION

Serve with vegetables, pepper sauce with meat / fish, peanut stew, Okro stew, beans etc

Meal

Green Pepper (Ofada) Sauce

Preparation time: 45 minutes
Cooking time: 40 minutes
Serves: 4-6

INGREDIENTS
- Assorted meats, dry fish, crayfish, stock fish etc
- Locust beans (fermented beans used in traditional African cooking) x half a cup
  (Use firm Locust beans – this is important in this recipe)
- Unripe tomatoes x 6
- Scotch Bonnet pepper x 1
- Sweet green peppers x 3
- Onions x 2
- Palm oil x 1 cup
- Salt and seasoning cubes (to taste)

METHOD OF COOKING
- Boil all the assorted meat and stock fish until tender, season well
- Add the dry fish and crayfish
- Grind the pepper, tomatoes and onions in a blender coarsely
- Heat up the palm oil in a big pan until bleached, allow to cool down
- Add all the pepper mixture and the locust beans (use firm locust beans, rinse thoroughly)
- Fire up the sauce, add all meat and fish, season to taste
- Stir at intervals.
- Cook for another 10-15 minutes

SERVING SUGGESTION
Serve with Ofada rice (unrefined / unpolished rice with distinct flavour) or any other rice,
bread, Sadza, Foofoo etc.

Jerk Chicken

Preparation time: 20 minutes
Cooking time: 30-40 minutes
Serves: 3-4

INGREDIENTS

- 6 Chicken fillets (or chicken on the bone)
- Ground allspice, thyme, x1 teaspoon
- Fresh garlic x 2 cloves crushed
- Onion x 1 small size, spring onion x a quarter cup chopped
- Ginger x 2 tablespoons grated
- Vinegar x half tablespoon
- Vegetable oil x 2 tablespoons
- Lime or lemon juice x half tablespoon
- Brown sugar (optional) x 2 teaspoons
- Scotch bonnet pepper or chilli to taste (chopped)
- Salt and ground black pepper to taste

METHOD OF COOKING

- Combine all the ingredients in a bowl to form a thick paste
- Make length way slits in the chicken
- Rub the marinade all over the chicken and into the slits
- Cover with clear film and marinate in the fridge overnight or for some hours
- Remove any excess marinade before cooking
- Brush the chicken with oil and place on the grill, BBQ or in the oven
- Cook for about 20-30 mins, turning at intervals (cook for longer if on the bone)

SERVING SUGGESTION

Serve with rice and peas, salad etc.

Chicken

Akara (Akaraje)

Pan Fried Bean Cake

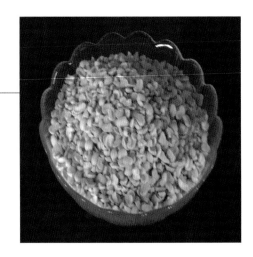

Preparation time: 45 minutes
Cooking time: 20 minutes
Serves: 6

INGREDIENTS
- Peeled black eye beans (soaked in water for about 25mins or until soft) x 2 cups
- Red sweet peppers x 1
- Medium sized onions x 2
- Scotch bonnet pepper or chilli x 1 (or to taste)
- Vegetable oil or palm oil x 2 cups
- Smoked African prawn or crayfish (ground) x 2 teaspoon (optional)
- Salt (to taste)
- Eggs (1 or 2) to bind, if necessary

METHOD OF COOKING
- Rinse the pre-soaked soft beans until clear (soft enough when it's easy to break)
- Peel onions, wash peppers
- Blend together the beans, peppers and onion in a liquidizer. Carefully add water to liquidize to a semi-stiff (not running at all) paste or consistency. Add finely diced onions (optional)
- Mix thoroughly and vigorously into a fluffy stiff paste (if too soft or watery add 1 or 2 eggs to bind)
- Add salt to taste
- Heat the oil up in a frying pan to very hot temperature
- Scoop the paste with a spoon lowering each scoop into the hot oil
- Allow to fry until golden or dark and crispy
- Drain excess oil on a kitchen towel or colander

NOTE – omit crayfish and shrimps for vegetarian or vegan option

SERVING SUGGESTION
Serve with bread, pap, kenkey or eat alone

(A k a r a j e)

Puff Puff

Preparation time: 45-60 minutes
Cooking time: 45 minutes
Serves: 6-8

INGREDIENTS
- Strong bread flour x 700g
- Fast acting baker's yeast x 7g
- 1 or 2 cups of sugar (adjust to taste)
- Spices (cinnamon / nutmeg /chilli) very optional
- Lukewarm water x 2 cups

METHOD OF COOKING
- In a big bowl, empty the flour and the sugar
- Make a little 'well' in the middle of the flour
- Add the yeast in the 'well'
- Pour the lukewarm water (about 36 degrees C), it has to be lukewarm. Not hot at all. This is to ensure the 'live' yeast is not killed
- Mix together into a smooth dough
- Cover the dough with a wet towel or cling film
- Keep in a warm place for about 30-45mins (a hot conservatory, room, or the airing cupboard)
- Allow to double in size
- Deep fry in sunflower oil

SERVING SUGGESTION
Serve piping hot or cold

Puff

Plantain (Fried)

Preparation time: 5 minutes
Cooking time: 10 minutes
Serves: 2-4

INGREDIENTS
- Ripe (yellow) plantain x 4
- Sunflower oil x 1 cup

METHOD OF COOKING
- Rinse the plantain under running water
- Cut both ends with knife (harder than opening a banana) and peel off the skin
- Cut into slices – not too thin
- Heat up some sunflower oil (palm oil or any vegetable oil) in a frying pan or any pan
- Shallow or deep fry the sliced plantain until golden brown (and not burnt!)
- Reduce the heat if shallow frying
- Drained into a kitchen towel and serve

SERVING SUGGESTION
Serve on its own or with rice, beans, ackee and fish, pepper sauce, fried eggs, beef or fish stew etc

(fried)

Plantain and Mixed Beans

Preparation time: 10 minutes
Cooking time: 15 minutes
Serves: 2-4

INGREDIENTS

- Ripe (yellow) plantain x 4
- Sunflower oil x 1 cup
- Mixed beans (cooked and canned) – red kidney, black eye beans and chick pea x 400g each
- Mixed peppers – one quarter of each colour
- Fresh Tomatoes (plum or vine) x 8
- Onions x 1 medium size
- Lettuce x 50g
- Herbs and spices x half a tablespoon mixed spices, 2 sprigs of fresh thyme
- Seasoning cubes and salt

METHOD OF COOKING

To fry the plantain

- Rinse the plantain under running water
- Cut both ends with a knife (harder than opening a banana) and peel off the skin
- Cut into slices – not too thin
- Heat up some sunflower oil (palm oil or any vegetable oil) in a frying pan or any pan
- Shallow or deep fry the sliced plantain until golden brown (and not burnt!)
- Reduce the heat if shallow frying
- Drain into a kitchen towel

For making the mixed beans

- Chop onions, mixed peppers and tomatoes (leaving some tomatoes for garnishing) and stir fry in about 2 tablespoons of oil for about 2 minutes
- Rinse all the beans and add to the stir fry mixture
- Season with the spices and herbs
- Finish off cooking after about 5 minutes
- Serve with plantain
- Garnish with lettuce and tomatoes

SERVING SUGGESTION

Serve on its own, or with rice, or as a complete meal especially for vegetarian or vegan choice.

Mixed Beans